www.blackriverart.com

Made in the USA
Monee, IL
12 May 2022

96301583R00103